The Pop Puffin

Maverick
Early Readers

D1385608

'The Pop Puffin'
An original concept by Jill Atkins
© Jill Atkins

Illustrated by Kelly Breemer

Published by MAVERICK ARTS PUBLISHING LTD
Studio 3A, City Business Centre, 6 Brighton Road,
Horsham, West Sussex, RH13 5BB
© Maverick Arts Publishing Limited August 2018
+44 (0)1403 256941

A CIP catalogue record for this book is available at the British Library.

ISBN 978-1-84886-362-0

www.maverickbooks.co.uk

Yellow

This book is rated as: Yellow Band (Guided Reading)
This story is decodable at Letters and Sounds Phase 3/4.

The Pop Puffin

by **Jill Atkins**

illustrated by **Kelly Breemer**

Puffin was fed up.

"I need to have fun," he said.

He ran to meet Gannet.

"I will be a pop singer," said Puffin.

"But you cannot sing," said Gannet.

"Yes, I can," said Puffin.

"Let me hear you," said Gannet.

"I can sing, too," said Gannet.

"I can sing, too," said Duck.

15

"I can sing, too," said Gull.

"We are all good," said Gannet.

"So let us all sing," said Puffin.

"I will tap my big feet," said Gannet.

"Me, too," said Puffin, Duck and Gull.

Tap, tap, tap, tap.

So all the birds sang and sang.

And it was a good pop song.

Puffin was happy!

"I am a pop puffin now," he said.

Quiz

1. What does Puffin want to do?

a) Be a pop singer

b) Be a dancer

c) Go to sleep

2. Who does Puffin talk to?

a) Cat

b) Dog

c) Gannet

3. And it was a _____ pop song.

a) Good

b) Bad

c) Fun

4. What do the birds do?

a) Fly around

b) Sing and tap their feet

c) Play games

5. What is Puffin?

a) A Dancing Puffin

b) A Flying Puffin

c) A Pop Puffin

Turn over for answers

Book Bands for Guided Reading

The Institute of Education book banding system is a scale of colours that reflects the various levels of reading difficulty. The bands are assigned by taking into account the content, the language style, the layout and phonics.

Maverick Early Readers are a bright, attractive range of books covering the pink to purple bands. All of these books have been book banded for guided reading to the industry standard and edited by a leading educational consultant.

Pink
Red
Yellow
Blue
Green
Orange
Turquoise
Purple
Gold
White

To view the whole Maverick Readers scheme, visit our website at
www.maverickearlyreaders.com

Or scan the QR code above to view our scheme instantly!

Quiz Answers: 1a, 2c, 3a, 4b, 5c